The Men from Praga

ANNE BERKELEY was born in Ludlow and grew up in Lincolnshire. Her pamphlet *The buoyancy aid and other poems* was published by Flarestack in 1997, and a selection of her work appeared in *Oxford Poets 2002* (Carcanet). She won the *TLS* prize in 2000 and was a prizewinner in the Arvon competition in 2004. She edited Rebecca Elson's acclaimed posthumous collection *A Responsibility to Awe* (Carcanet, 2001) and is currently editor of the poetry journal *Seam*. She is one of the poetry group Joy of Six, with whom she has performed across the UK and in New York.

The Men from Praga

ANNE BERKELEY

CAMBRIDGE

PUBLISHED BY SALT PUBLISHING
14a High Street, Fulbourn, Cambridge CB21 5DH United Kingdom

© Anne Berkeley 2009

The right of Anne Berkeley to be identified as the
author of this work has been asserted by her in accordance
with Section 77 of the Copyright, Designs and Patents Act 1988.

Salt Publishing 2009

Printed in the UK by the MPG Books Group

Typeset in Swift 9.5 / 13

ISBN 978 1 84471 422 3 paperback

Salt Publishing Ltd gratefully acknowledges
the financial assistance of Arts Council England

1 3 5 7 9 8 6 4 2

Contents

Acknowledgements

Some of these poems first appeared in *Oxford Poets 2002* (Carcanet Press), *Flirtation* (Mainsail Press, 2002) and *A clock-storm coming* (Cinnamon Press, 2006).

Other poems, or earlier versions of them, have appeared in *The Interpreter's House*, *Madingley Poems*, *Oxford Poetry*, *Smiths Knoll*, *Reactions*, *The Rialto*, *Tabla* and *The Times Literary Supplement*.

'The Men from Praga' won first prize in the *TLS* competition, 2000. 'Hold-all (*Aircrew*)' was a prizewinner in the Arvon competition, 2004. 'Gasometer' was a prizewinner in the *Tabla* competition, 2000.

Thanks are due to Sheenagh Pugh and other staff and fellow students at The University of Glamorgan, and to my colleagues and friends in Joy of Six and First Tuesday, and at the Mary Ward workshop. I am also grateful to the Trustees of The Hawthornden Trust for the granting of a Fellowship in 2004 during which time many of these poems were written or revised.

I Co-ordinates

We have got to have this thing over here, whatever it costs . . .
we have got to have a bloody Union Jack on top of it . . .

ERNEST BEVIN, *Foreign Secretary*, 1946

Hold-all (*Aircrew*)

You served to carry my father's civvies,
spare flying rations, pressure-suit, presents.
You brought us tangerines fresh from the tree.

After each tour of duty, you suffered
being flung on the floor, skidding on metal feet,
and slumped there, heavy as a body.

If you ever glimpsed the Vulcan's purpose
above the clouds as you rode in the bomb-bay,
you held your peace.

From the childhood of your ID tag
you reproach me with mute loyalty,
your two handles like ears, waiting for orders.

Forgive me, you were always too heavy
with dirty laundry and official secrets.
I was never allowed to touch you.

Let me take some weight from you now.
Let me listen to the long yawn of your zip
as you spill out your puzzling odours

and I will try not to resent your shared journeys,
the long absences and whispers, the crises.
Unpack for me again the doll from Malta,

panpipes from Nicosia and tangerines from Tripoli,
still with their leaves, still cold from 50,000 feet.
Even empty, I doubt I can carry you.

Vapour Trail

Lincolnshire's in shadow. My father leaves the plain
in screams of light. He navigates
high over maps and mountains with names
I can't pronounce. Gold a micron thick laminates the glass.

His slide rule shuttles on his knees.
He's gone beyond a point of light. There's only noise.

Through rose-tinted glass the pilot shadows mountains,
cities, a great river winding through the plain.
The navigator with his slide-rule can't see out
but crouches at the radar-sweep within arm's reach of the light.

Yellow Sun, Green Grass

When I lived in my father's house
The Bomb was mighty and ruled over the earth
And the Bomb was a mystery
And my father was its servant
And the names of the Bomb were secret and unspoken

The Bomb was in the sky and came down to earth
To bring peace to the world

And these were some of the names of the Bomb in those days:
    Blue Danube, Green Grass, Yellow Sun, Red Snow
And they were forbidden to be spoken
And the Bomb was hidden

The Government praised the Bomb
And the people made sacrifices
For the Bomb gave us strength
For the Bomb kept us safe

And those who cursed the Bomb gave succour to our enemies
And we despised them

When the Bomb went forth the earth trembled and the
      heavens were rent
And the heavens wept
And the Bomb would come again

I lived in fear of the Bomb
I dreamed I lived and looked on the terrible face of the Bomb

Flat 9

When I googled it, I was afraid
to disturb my carefully-tended myth
that dozed in court, gazebo, balustrade,
labyrinths that nothing real compares with.

Back when we knew it, the house appeared to us
from fragments of someone else's dream
we trod, but didn't understand because
we were small and thought only children dreamed,

so we rampaged through it, having other uses
for things we loved but didn't recognise —
patchy, mossed, forgotten grown-up stuff

like the brambly garden with stone muses,
dry fountains catching nothing from blue skies,
and a broken sundial with time enough.

Revesby

The ballroom is kept shuttered. No one has the key.
Roll-eyed carvings guard the stairs—what's the password?—
mirrors echo in the hall, mahogany and vast.
No Ballgames on the Parterre. I told on them, so I'm a spy.

When the gang's coming after me, I scramble
into the straggly box hedge, and watch them searching.
The knot-garden's tangled, a cat's-cradle gone wrong.
My parents say you must learn to make new friends.

Stone ladies in the garden bare their breasts and bottoms
through the bones of a pergola like a broken tomb.
They show off hooks from elbows, orange scabs.
I need a cap-gun, I said, to defend myself.

Once, I hid inside an empty fountain,
staring at the green thing in the middle and willing it to gush.
Dried moss scratched my arms. A Vulcan screamed, so low
it made the twisted chimneys faint. I could have touched it.

No, I never hear *The Blue Danube*, the carriages at dawn.
There's no such thing as ghosts. The others will be waiting
on the backstairs with their skipping-ropes and helmets
to escort me to the basement, where the rats run free.

The Boasts of Jim McKay

Wyatt Earp
longest burp
furthest hitter
best spitter
worst chickenpox
biggest, strongest, oldest, boss

Tonto the white rat
proper Davy Crockett hat
calls his mother *Mum* not *Mummy*
one whole shilling pocket money

a kilt, which isn't sissy if you're Scottish
fifty pounds in the Post Office
a real working watch
Hogmanay, St Andrew's Day
knife in his sock

a gang and a den
Jim McKay and his Merry Men
box of matches and a cigarette
Scalextric set

never cries
cut off your tongue and boil your eyes
till they burst
see up your skirt

a six inch scar
when he'd crashed his uncle's racing-car
at two hundred miles an hour

been up the Eiffel Tower
eats fried brains

needs stitches again
none of your business
will get a bike for Christmas

the boss of you the boss of this school the boss of the whole world
a boy is always better than a girl

The Old Arboretum

There were strange cones in the woods, and pale leaves
that smelt of medicine. Bushes with red berries
they told us not to pick. There were bamboos
we made bows and arrows with, or spears.

We shot at pigeons in the chestnuts, but never got one.
We made fires and cooked apples in a billycan.
We always covered up our poo with leaves.

We played conkers and Jim McKay threw sticks to get them
    down.
One hit me on the lip—I needed stitches.
Once he threw me in the nettles—that was worse.

Jim McKay owned a treehouse, in the biggest cedar.
They just took it—my favourite tree.
And they cheated and put in footholds.
It isn't proper climbing if you use nails.
I told him, it's not a proper treehouse if your father builds it.
Even with stepladder and trapdoor.
I could climb any tree I wanted, higher than him.

Then there was the time he chased me
up the tree that only I could climb.
He was older and heavier, so only got half way,
shouting. He tried to shake me off. I shinned
to where the trunk was thinner than my wrist—
however much he shook, I would not let go.
Better than a fairground ride, I said.
Then laughed. He didn't like that. I wasn't *really* scared.
He couldn't kill me, because he'd get into trouble.

He said he'd say it was an accident.

His mother called him in for tea.
I watched him go, ginger hair bobbing as he ran.
I leaned against the branch. I didn't cry.
A clear shot from my perch, if I had an arrow.

My Mother's Migraines

I'm running up and down the landing till the noise
bounces off the panelling behind the statues
even when I've stopped sometimes on wet days
Diana rides her bike here you're not supposed to say bike
it's bicycle it's one of those long words like
telephone and television which we haven't got
and refrigerator it's just arrived I keep
opening the door to see the light and you can make
ice-cream which is jolly good because next week
it's my birthday my present's a surprise
I want a gun but I won't get a bike
until I'm ten and that is years and years and years away

Small Arms

Two fingers, bang bang, don't make a gun
when everyone's got rolls of caps
and a tree-house to defend. You run
whooping with a pigeon feather
to loose flaming arrows at Wyatt Earps
but they're playing a different game,
where they shoot you dead and you can't shoot back.
They stamp on your fingers when you attack
the ladder of their fort. It isn't fair. It hurts.
You only wanted to join in. You run away.

Next day, you're one year older.
Doc Birthday. Your gun's brand new.
It's silver and mother o'pearl,
so heavy, it takes both hands to aim.
Too big for your pocket or the holster
you don't have. Too long to twirl
but there's a hundred caps, blood blisters
in a waxed box, bang and smoke
and air that rings and blurs and tastes of blue.

The shoot-out leaves you light-headed,
exhausted, penniless,
an empty barrel's click.
Dead eye. Ha-ha, missed.

This gun's useless now. Fling it down.
It was a real gun you wanted most,
a real gun to shoot them dead
so now you resurrect yourself, tear through
their haze of bullets, unharmed, like a ghost.

Russkis

I am a spy
creeping about the landing
behind the statues
disguised as a Mexican
listening at doors

Morse code's tapping
along the gutter

Mrs McKay's hoover
could be a cover
for a hidden telephone

Words can shrink
and fly through wires

The Americans
have blocked up their keyhole
to guard their music
They're not speaking English

I saw the postman on the stairs
the letters for No 11
had foreign stamps

By the pantry door
was a cast of mud
from the gunman's boot

When the weather clears
I will look for letters
in the hollow
of the old conker tree

Sputnik will track me
so I wear a big hat
to hide my face
from the man-made moon

The Americans

She has a new baby.
I don't like babies
but she asked me to tea.

Mummy said Go
and mind your Ps
and Qs, young lady.

She shows me the photo
of her husband in Cyprus.
He's a policeman for NATO.

She has a radiogram.
And Coca Cola.
And peanut butter.

She offers me jelly
—it's strawberry jam.
I say jelly's for parties.

The baby's too small to play.
It just sleeps
and sometimes it cries.

She asks me questions:
Do I miss my father?
I don't know the right answer.

The Balcony

Just for show, they say, *to crown the entrance,*
not for standing on. Be quick. The one sash, in the middle,
so narrow no one else can wriggle through.
Don't lean over, don't look down. Of course, I do.

I hand in his Austin Healey, chipped Aston Martin,
then stay out there awhile tormenting them,
enjoying the air, the tiny gravel far below,
the slightly altered view across the deerpark.

And when, following its long rumour,
Sqn Ldr Belcher's brand new Humber
first comes hushing round the bend in the drive,
they order me back in. But I know what I should do.

I wave. A hiding's coming anyway, so
I wave and wave, slowly, like the Queen.

Downstairs

The basement's out of bounds.
It isn't safe. There are rats.
There isn't anything to see.
The backstairs are kept locked
behind the door with bobble glass.
You want to see, though. You want to see.

You want the dizzy spiral stairs,
the curve of walls and a new way down.
You want to see the basement. The dungeon.
You want to see a real live rat.

Just this once then.
He gets a torch, a stick, the key.
The wall is speckled green, like ice-cream in the gutter.
The stairs are plain unpolished wood
down to the basement, where the smell comes from.

Down there, the ceiling's low. It's dark and cold.
This is where the bells ring
from the buttons upstairs you're not allowed to touch.
There's no one here. No prisoners. No treasure.
Only damp, and crunchy plaster, old sinks, broken tiles.
And a rat in torchlight, scrabbling from a shelf—
Perhaps you never see the rat, only hear it.
Perhaps you only ever hear about the rat.

The rooms go on forever. You could get lost
underneath the hall, the ballroom, the Wing Commander's
       flat.
The basement holds the whole house up.
It connects to everything. And it's empty.

You're just a little child, you know nothing.
You're not guilty yet.
History's just a building where you live.

We could play down here when it's raining.
No, he says. No.
Perhaps you never see the basement.
We're not supposed to be down here.
Perhaps you never tell a soul.

Olympus Mk 301

The camp was strung with bunting.
A brass band filled the corners of the afternoon.
Men in uniform saluted us. We stood around
while the mothers talked, and I had to be polite.
And I couldn't have an ice cream, or a seat.

As the crew went up the ladder
we stood behind the rope and waved.
I couldn't run to him: we had to stay
just where we were. This was his job.
In his flying kit, he did not belong to us.

Too far away to really see his face,
like those bedtimes when a point of light
scored the evening sky
and I knew he'd look down and see me wave—
but nearer than I'd ever been before
to the black holes where the turbines span
heat and noise that made the airfield wobble, faint—

Not just noise
but a whole-body shockwave. The hurt kept coming
and wouldn't stop. Hands against my ears couldn't shut it out.
They opened up the throttle.
I lay on the ground and howled.
The grass itself was shaking in the awful wind.

And as they lifted off
and wheels folded in and lost themselves
I felt the noise would swallow him
and all of us and never stop.

Was I smacked? I expect so.
Don't be silly darling, Daddy works with noise all day.
So this was the special thing he did,
what he'd been trained for:
holding steadfast with the noise
to leave the solid ground from the runway
and change into a point of light
to cross the heavens spreading noise
a great cone of noise
to spill across the face of the earth.

Night Sky in October

For days we scanned the sky for planes
but they never came.
Jim McKay saw a UFO, though,
from up the top field behind the pig shed.
Next night, a dozen of us went to look: held
our breath against the downwind stink, waited
for his 'slim cigar-tube, one end glowing red'
to emerge from Ursa Major,
containing god-knows-what . . .
It was daft to think of polished metal cylinders
out-sized, un-screwtopped, un-dented, and not
spilling fishing-floats, drill-bits, pipe-cleaners.
Still, even stars start twitching if you stare long enough
chin up, downwind, holding your breath.

Bunker

I

It was wrong of me

The bunker was there
under the green hill
as big as my guilt

controlling
the remnants of army
the heavens laid waste

and me in my bunker

drinking bottled water
eating canned peas
shouting orders

No one should know
about the bunker
only the Prime Minister
and senior civil servants
some handpicked soldiers

a telephone
an iron bed

and troops outside
in leaden suits
and visors
shooting the looters
can touch nothing
can eat nothing
who got our wish granted
like King Midas

When I grow up
I want to be
a soldier
or a senior civil servant
or Prime Minister

they would do their duty
from the bunker
their bounden duty
shuttling magnetic markers
on maps
no longer resembling the world

After my father had done his duty
they would do theirs

II

It was wrong
to want to survive

because it was selfish
because surviving was terrible
because of the burns
because of the desert
because of no air
because of nothing left
my darling, you cannot begin to imagine

But that doesn't stop me
or the dreams

I am in the control tower
the horizon vanishes
in the light of creation
elemental rearrangement
chain reaction
it is blinding white
then golden
I am see-through
then the shockwave
kicks me back

I want to see to the very end
because I cannot imagine

only enough
to frighten myself
not enough
to control it

If I could command
wreak vengeance on mine enemies

O who am I
that can hate so much

down in my bunker

But what would be the point
if you could never go out

if something you'd done
changed the world for ever

not just for you
for everyone

everyone who was left

III

I walked down the street—no
The sun rose over the meadow—no
such precious things

Even the dustcart
men shouting across the street
as they haul the bins
become tiny
unrepeatable

It was in the days
before dayglo
before wheelie bins
when the dustcart
carried its ordure
like a vast bureau

IV

What, can you
love even cockroaches
for being alive?

Might the last man
embrace a mossy rock:
cousin, cousin!

Even to imagine
is a sin:
how could you,
how could you think such things?

As for
ever wanting

only with the greatest sorrow

the tears of the Prime Minister
so comic-book it's embarrassing

no alternative

anyway it's a lie
about cockroaches

V

And that's another thing:
the child who sang
the child who was taught
sing this, not that

do what the others . . .
(the others wait, smirking)
the others . . .

it felt like death

to surrender
the singing self
to the chant
two twos are four

VI

I don't want to hug
my inner child
I want to strangle
the sodding brat

who will always tug
my clean white sleeve

and I have to lug her
everywhere
her weight, her weight

Nav Rad

The Vulcan beat out such a din
there's heavy irony
in the imagery
of anvil and sickle.
Heaven 'd
weep at what my father knew:
co-ordinates
of targets,
the precise skill
of Blue Steel
to raze so many by so few—
returning with his burden
red-eyed, limping, deafened
by a damaged ossicle.

Co-ordinates

Last year, when a friend sent him a postcard from Odessa,
it was the first time he'd ever seen pictures of the city:
the Opera House, and a broad flight of steps
peopled in the sunshine with descendants of the enemy.

II Trajectories

The Men from Praga

Because my Polish doesn't run to 'tram ticket',
I have to walk. And my camera's jammed.
I jab it with my gloves. Brush at orange grit
the wind flings off the tarmac. It's miles.
And anyway, the light's gone.

Over the bridge, across the Vistula, is Praga—
the Bear Pit, the badlands, the concrete tower blocks.
The sky weighs down on the river, beats it flat,
squeezing out the scum that snags on reeds.
I imagine heavy industries upstream.

But it isn't scum. Ice. Its visible edge. Because,
down on the river, far from shore,
two men crouch on camp-stools, hauling
something in from the tricky gleam, doing
intricate, delicate things with their bare hands.

I watch them. They're quite at home
out there in the channel. Smoking, fixing bait.
The wind flicks Polish at me. It's all beyond me—
their Sunday morning ease, their ice,
the fluent fish at large below their feet.

River

His deep voice gets you up in the morning,
always in a hurry, no time for nonsense.

In his grubby string vest he muscles down the valley,
singing loudly, sweeping away all objections.
At night you hear his murmur, grownup through floorboards.

His temper is huge but predictable.
He always knows where he's going. When thwarted,
knows no bounds. Then you need
oilskins, gumboots, a quick boat out of town.

Sometimes he'll bring you a surprise: fish,
a little canoe, a dragonfly. He keeps
a kingfisher up his sleeve for nostalgia.
Sometimes there'll be algae for days.
He says nothing about the drowned kittens.

You cannot fathom him: if you ever find
your own reflection in him, it will be very small.
A long way back, another river joined him; her name was lost
          in his.

He works down at the mill, strong and dependable.
People stop to watch, impressed by his power, his easy grace
with the battling wheel. You are proud of him then.

Now, the dredgers have come.
He sits scared and stiff after the operation.
So grey and quiet in his narrow bed, you hardly dare look.
No swans for weeks.

A Portrait of V Nubiola

His red jacket buttons up a fury of muscle
Everything's on the point of change
Only the soft popping of his lips as they draw on his pipe
the engine of desire
He leans his elbow on the table to stop it collapsing
to maintain the balance between two apples
He is furiously smoking to hold aloft
the miraculous circle, the *memento mori*
that hovers between pipe and decanter
Even the tulip leans away, about to take flight

I go into the room to straighten the table leg
The heat is unbearable
I ask him, what do you do when you're not sitting here
holding this impossible bubble in the air?
What debt do you owe, that you consent
to illustrate the Principle of Moments?
He cannot speak for the pipe
If he grips any harder the stem will snap
So long as he keeps smoking
his jacket will stay red, his rooftiles
will shrug off hailstones
and his hands will keep from necks and knives

When I come out again bearing the decanter
I unstopper it and smell—rough stuff
from down the southern end of the winelake
The sort that doesn't travel
I realise how much depends on him

I leave behind the two apples
One has a bad bruise on the side I can't see
The other, on closer inspection
isn't an apple at all

Boots

The shoeshine boy
at the foot
of the man in the coat

kneels to wax
as if over tinder
coaxing a gleam

and now the black
velvet strop
blurs and
sharpens the light

till the boot
surfaces

Should the man stoop
to look
he'd see the spit
image of himself

Thirsty

The A1 near Alconbury Weston,
heading north

after the choke of the A14—
half of busy Europe tramping from
Felixstowe to Birmingham
in the wake of the slowest
frigorifique's exhaust—

now you're gulping miles so pure, so vast and empty
your car's a Maserati.

And long before Sawtry, in a sweet
draught of flowering beans, the verges white
with ox-eyed daisies, you're swallowing the whole
Nene Valley: church spires, floodplain, light industrial;

your roof and road wide open, the sky's constant blue
music all that's keeping pace with you.

Accident

One moment you're upright, in charge
of your life, your bike, the lot
but a little thing can make you wobble off
you know, a leak or something,
a puncture,
some rent in the fabric of a normal morning
through which a car door opens or the sun over-
takes a rear-view mirror,
so suddenly everything stops
and notices:
are you all right Mrs?
and in the innocent blue day
there's a puddle by the pedal and you hear yourself say,
Perfectly, yes, thank you,
and straighten through your cramp
both front and back of your damp
skirt, and someone says, look here (kindly) you'd better
see a doctor
so you can choose then to be grateful
and the normal chintz or clockface rips a little more,
with a noise this time, like a moan in a blanket
though you're too hot, it's so hot,
and easier to be absent from the blood that's not
happening to you but like all these others,
who are they, you're watching
and your back hurts and maybe your entire body
is borne up on gears of pain
like migraine lights and interrogation
until you're on your bike again
but naked, and the pedals won't go round
and a madman with a knife is shouting
from underneath you in a mint-green gown
Stop screaming will you Mrs . . .
shut your mouth damn you and push—
I push, I push, I push, uphill all the bloody way.

Taking the Air

Let's go to the carp pond—
there's supposed to be
a kingfisher—

But out in the open, heat
smacks us, sudden as grief.
The willow tree's an unstruck bell.
Under it we dare not speak.

Glance at the sun,
a purple wound:
and you're scarred for hours,
a hole in everywhere you look.

Displaced sky
flicks in and out of vision,
twitches on the reed-mace:
damselflies dismantling food.
Water broods on its mud.

Sounds fall into place: clockwork croak,
crickets' ratchet,
leaf rattle and echo.
We are losing the summer.

Pigeons clatter, far off.
Swallows cuff the water.
There is nothing
to mistake for a kingfisher.

Grounded creatures, without wings
or occupation,
we stare at water milky as tea,
shy of sharing a hurt.

The carp are there, somewhere,
just under the surface.

Advice from Nils

Day follows day, you realise,
right up until the sunset
that draws a dotted line

so you can cut it off and drink to it
as it fades on the sofa. Then,
you know, is the best time of all,

this is how to live. And
with your filleting-knife
(re-folded in your pocket)

slit open its glittering belly,
slide it into the pan
to eat with a fresh loaf.

Nils Takes a Breather

I need somewhere private to write it down:
onscreen even a moment, there's a trace.

So I practise lines to fit a Rizla,
slope into the yard with my roll-up
to open my mouth in the icy rain
and let slip your name, your name.

Two fingers up for the CCTV.
Just an old addict, airing his lungs.
A misleading breath, a sleight of the tongue

escapes in its Montgolfier bubble
with forged identification papers.
I wave it off, and set back to work, work,

grappling with keyboard and accounts,
the mind still at odds with the hands.

Baudelaire's Pipe

I

Stroke
my Abyssinian hip:
I'm an experienced pipe—
a real writer's smoke.

When his spirits ache
my chimney fires up
like a home where good soup
greets the ploughman from work.

I embrace
and rock him idle
in my gauzy blue cradle,

whispering peace
in fragrant loops
from my passionate lips.

II

after Babelfish*

I am the pipe of a writer;
one sees, contemplating my mien,
Abyssinian or Cafrine,
that my master abuses his lighter.

When he's felled with pain,
I smoke like the cottage
where steaming pottage
awaits the homecoming swain.

I weave and I lull his soul
in the motile blue lace
that climbs from my mouth in fire,

and the powerful balm I roll
charms his spirit with grace
that lifts his heart from the mire.

* Babelfish (www.babelfish.com) is an online automatic translation tool,
named after the fish in Douglas Adams's *The Hitch-hiker's Guide to the
Galaxy*

[46]

III

I am the pipe of a writer;
you can tell from my complexion
he's held me in affection
since his teeth were whiter.

When he's feeling depressed
I'll be cooking the dinner
for the weary breadwinner
coming home for a rest.

I practise my charm
in flimsy blue laces,
with fragrant embraces,

and powerful balm
for the shift he must crave
from master to slave.

IV

I'm a writer's pipe
and I know my place,
my African face
his stereotype.

When his spirits droop
I'm the labourer's hut
where supper's hot
and I warm his lap,

then I tie him well
in lacy net
with a blue slipknot

and utter a spell
over my pet
in his oubliette.

V

I'm a poet's toke
tanned
in the hand
of an addict to smoke.

When things get him down
I'm the familiar chimney pot,
his something hot,
bath, slippers and dressing-gown.

I hold sway
in a blue
lasso

till he's well away,
off his face
in my embrace.

VI

I'm an author's pipe;
you can see from my face
the dominant race
buys that nicotine hype.

When he's feeling sore,
I pretend to cook
in a cosy nook
like a ganger's whore

and I rock his heart
in the blues I weave
when hot lips pucker

and my nebulous art
seems to relieve
the miserable fucker.

A Change in the Weather
(after Hugo)

Go home, spits the north wind
This is my aria—
and I'm shaken:
my crestfallen

song daren't contend
with a prima donna,
it's overwhelmed
by scorn.

Rain. It's the chorus-line
kiss-off, whatever the song.
The show's over, swallows.
Time we were gone.

Hail and wind. Wrench
of withered branches.
Against slate sky
smoke flits, white.

The hillside shivers
under skimpy gold leaf.
My fingers flinch
from the keyhole's breath.

Vacant Possession

It's time
we had a chat, house.

House, I used to think
meant *roof, walls, a kettle in the kitchen.*

I dressed you
in paint, adept with plaster and splint.

I've nursed you
through drought and thunderstorm, holding tight.

With my own fingers
I've cleared the gutter's throat, throttled a burst pipe.

I've forgiven
your other life: the rosebud of wasps' nest, the silverfish

and you have forgiven
my intolerance of wallpaper, the promise broken in the
        conservatory —

but there's a place
in the corner of the bedroom that never gets warm

there are whole rooms
I ignore for weeks on end —

and yet at night
I dream of attics and cellars you've never had

so come clean, house,
about these rooms standing bare waiting for tenants.

I can almost see
doorways knocked through,

a new aspect
of fields from the hallway, clouds over the landing.

I never knew
you wanted to be a tent, an airship—

Was there ever a time
when I faced you squarely,

listened
to the heave and sigh of your possibilities?

Matthew Crampton

Matthew Crampton lived for a glimpse of heaven—
twenty years in poverty on a hilltop,
every morning praying for light or weather,
washed in the dewpond.

He prepared his soul as he fed the chickens,
hoed the stones, recorded his every scraping;
every evening prayed and untied his sandals,
wrote in his diary.

Came the year when snow never left the mountains.
Seedcorn finished, cannibal bantams, he wrote,
nothing for it now but to show them mercy,
twisted their heads off.

Firewood all gone, furniture, feathers—Matthew
burned his diary, lay on the mattress-shadow
on his left side, facing the only window,
watching the sunset.

Pauahi Crater 10 a.m.

I give you this space: the rock at your feet
suddenly gaping. Six hundred paces
of empty air, or air so full of morning
that distance faints. A space full of the years
since its catastrophe, a space of shadow
where, if you fell, you could count seconds down.
Green—perhaps ferns, perhaps ohia trees,
so small, so far away, beyond shouting.

But this pit is full of invisible light
that cannot sing if nothing echoes it.
Nothing can give it shape or scale, until
a white-tailed tropicbird rises into
diagonal volume, trails streamers through
from blossom to star-pink blossom.

Between the Twenty-sixth
and the Twenty-seventh Floors

Between floors I'd take the backstairs
even in winter,
to save waiting all evers for the lift.
And there, in the drift
of night-cleaners' ganja,
alone with the unheated
ghosts of fire-drills,
my heels
loud on the bare concrete,
the thought of you would catch me unawares

against the flow, lift me off my feet—
memos and agenda proofs
clattering around me in a shower—you'd take me
to the view from the roof.
Then after twenty steps, I'd have to key
back to carpets
and fluorescent lights,
the low hum
and Dixon
standing up to the telephone,
shirtsleeved elbow
busy, scratching, and I'd go to the window
and once or twice, below me,
a snowstorm swaggered down Victoria Street.

Chattel

I must have lent it to a client:
that little grunt people make after signing
must have been the last I knew
of its slick gilt snuggled in someone's paw
who palmed it as talk turned to the future.

Or it sleeps
in a closed book,
a placeholder in *De Voil's Law and Practice of VAT.*

My sixth finger, my forked tongue.
It must exist somewhere.
Someone must have it. Not a magpie or cat burglar.
Not dropped through a drain, a crack in space-time.
No. Some bugger has it.
I wish him joy of it.

Let him lift the nib to his nose
for that mouth-filling St Emilion gust of ink.
Let him squint to decode the hallmarks.
Let him relive hours doodled in the Administration Committee,
love letters, cheques,
delight in its shuffle across the page.
Let him take care of the pinch in the bladder
as he recharges from the murk.
Let him draw satisfaction from the small daily ceremonies
of capping and uncapping, business as usual,
a man of property.
Let it remind him of a grandmother in a navy hat,
proud of his success.
And when it writes, let it run clear, without blot or stain
to tell it true. *This is my act and deed. This is my name.*

Britannia

Careful not to soil her dainty Ferragamos,
the grand piano moves discreetly through the herbaceous border,
a sheaf of cuttings in her handbag:
a cardinal, the Queen's gynaecologist, a dozen QCs.

She has come for the music, of course,
but the atmosphere's lovely, such elegant lampshades.
There is always some Government in the garden
where the sheep are kept in their rightful place
safely grazing beyond the haha.

There are twenty-two minutes before curtain up.
The wind is cold, there's a whimper of rain
but the picnic must go on and be such fun:
an open window serves coloratura with paté de foie gras.
Everyone has a rug for their knees, and she reminds us
again of her night at the Albert Hall,
the swallowing blue of a million delphiniums.
We can almost believe in her cloak-pin and shield.

It's not what it was, she says: the vulgar new building,
every year the path to the lily pond more overgrown—
a negotiation of unripened blackberries and birtwistle.
Hemlines are rising; already accountants wash up on the lawn.

Even today, out at sea with Johnny Foreigner,
I hear her triumphant arpeggios over the waves,
the Broadwood's fin patrolling round the violins.

They

Sleep's a fragile thing—a sound is dying—
bark like muntjac gone before you've heard it,
reminding you of something, like a conscience.

The vixen and owl ignore our roads,
our ways of thinking. They have their own
maps and reasons for their screams.

Out there with them in the dark, up to no good,
down the other path, sniffing at the hazel bush,
running perhaps, careful not to let the dry stick snap

or the latch click on the hencoop or the car
door slam twice, the stray thoughts,
disowned for crimes of being

right or wrong or inconsolable
hunt and couple and redouble.
You must know something of this

staring through wiped windows in the dark
into another train that isn't there, another set of eyes
focusing through yours into the rain. You'd think

they'd come running on a wet November evening,
when streetlamps gather haloes of wet twigs,
they'd edge round light from study windows, watching.

They never answer when I call them
through the emptied spaces.
I've never seen them, but I know they're there.

Call them our drathers and our failures,
our esprits de l'escalier, it's not they who have escaped.
Their day will come. They know how they outnumber us.

One Way of Listening to Windchimes

1

During the small hours in Oundle
the only moving thing
was the set of windchimes.

2

It lodged in my mind
like a tree
in which there are windchimes.

3

The windchimes whirled in the autumn winds.
They were small windchimes in the pandemonium.

4

A man and a woman
are one.
A man and a woman and windchimes
are not.

5

I do not know which is worse,
the pitch of windchimes
or the dissonance of windchimes,
the windchimes chiming
or just before.

6

Windchimes filled the long window
with soprano windchimes.
The echo of windchimes
crossed it to and fro.
The effect
traced in the echo
an unrepeatable word.

7

O fat woman of Blackpot Lane
why do you hang windchimes?
Do you not hear how silence
could walk among your begonias?

8

I know the laws of nuisance
and lucid, unmistakeable arguments.
But I know, too,
that the windchimes are involved
in what I know.

9

When the windchimes are out of earshot
I know I am far from home.

10

At the sound of windchimes
plinging past midnight
the next door neighbours
are sleeping sweetly.

11

He drove to Peterborough
in an old car.
Once, a panic stabbed him,
in that he mistook
the police siren
for windchimes.

12

The air is moving.
The windchimes must be chiming.

13

It has been summer all afternoon.
There is a light breeze
and there is going to be a thunderstorm.
The windchimes hang
from the apple tree.

Food for Scandal

The blind cook always has clean hands.
He thumbs the blade before shaving
the marinated salmon so thin
you could read the paper through it.

With his mezzaluna
he rocks windowsill chives
into jittering crumbs, parts
the coriander's womanish smell.

The gas whispers and soughs: its heat
feels for his face. He sets the skillet
to sizzle citruses, soy, olive oil;
attends the fragrant spattering.

He arranges the salmon, the picked
white crabmeat, the clashing herbs
and shredded scallions; calculates sauce;
adds a wafer of pickled ginger;

and before serving, wipes the rim
with a clean napkin; bears
a plate in each hand, out to his dining room
where the curtains are drawn and the candles lit.

Gasometer

I used to run past Gas Street, afraid
the merest whim would spark it off. It loomed green
over everything, the garlic smell warning
of strange powers. It went up and down
like moods, the whole town lit up and cooking.

The North Sea bubble blew it out.
Around the country, empty gantries lingered
beyond notice on the skyline, rusting and redundant,
to be wrenched apart by economic forces,
oxy-torches and an engine with a shear.

Which is why I'm up here, nose-down on this dome
where they're peeling back the skin: rivet-dimpled,
with blooms of colour where the torch has cut.
Paint flakes and catches underneath my nails.
Unconcealed, the tank goes deeper than I'd thought.

The edge I'm leaning on creaks slightly
but it's warm in the sun as my camera gropes
for the secrets of its structure, how in the dark
it swelled with power on a raft of water and floated up
to the very top. This broken, empty thing—I want

it whole again, the spokes and posts re-covered
as the welders left them, sealed under me and rising . . .
Guide wheels squeak up pillars and in the yard
they're shovelling coke, and gas is filling darkness
half an inch below me, lifting me into the view.

Great Lettuce in The Botanic Garden

There is music, and tinkling of glasses.

Gatecrashers,
subversives parachuted in,
bide their time
under the feathery shade
of *sophora japonica*.
Tall enough to pass as background,
they lean out in unison to the path,
slender, understated in the season's colours,
guarding their spikes under their leaves.
They'll use them if they have to.
They open their packed damage
slowly, let it drift on the wind
to follow the programme.
Filaments barely interrupt sight.

And still the men arrive for the garden party
sporting boaters, linen jackets, cravats.
Their ladies chatter in floaty dresses,
catalpa and poppy, hebe and tilia.

My Backyard

They're breaking up the yard
JCB, pneumatic drill
breaking up the yard

toe-tectors, ear defenders, shorts
breaking up the yard that floods in the rain
they're breaking up the yard and they sweat in their labour

mechanical digger jabbers and hammers
the surface where things appeared
Jehovah's Witnesses, Tory canvassers

furniture letters milk
birch leaves willow leaves frost
my stretch of skin-of-the-earth stripped away
the place we stood and kissed

they are breaking up the yard
bootsoles and tyres
they are wiping the tape of our feet
they are breaking up the yard and the whole house shakes
I feel it in my bones
they are breaking up the yard and the whole world shakes

and all round the world they are breaking up yards
they are breaking down walls
they are bulldozing factories to the ground
wiping out shanties, cracking houses like eggs
and all the shelters and hedges and forests and yards

they are breaking up the yard
they are breaking up the yard and the whole house shakes
they are breaking up the yard and carting it away

Landless

They don't know I'm in here.
If they ever find tracks, scrabbled earth, rabbit's blood,
they think 'cat'.
Muffled in fog, I sharpen my knife,
wipe out the ash with the ball of my foot,
drink before dawn from the gardeners' tap.
The heir wanted wildlife—
well, he's got me.

            I vanish through shadows,
raiding the bins, after a banquet eat like a king,
buy time from the dogs at the Mews with a bone.
When the standard's unfurled, I keep to the trees.
The guards watch the wall for intruders and bombs.
With their greatcoats and coffee, they'll never see me.

Spring comes with birds' eggs, and wild orchid roots.
But I don't kid myself—this isn't the wild.
High walls and spikes, soldiers and dogs:
the heart of the city in a country gone mad.

Rumour blows in over the wall, newspaper scraps.
I catch what I can. They pin it twice daily
to barrow away. They're frightened of birds.
They're numbering souls. They're locking up
people like me. Tomorrow: light flurries of snow.

I lie under the twigs that cross out the sky,
the yellowing night robbed of its stars.
Beyond the high walls, a long tawny roar.
The city so close, like a radio.
I can't tune it out.
Closer than that.

What frightens me most
isn't sickness or frost
but the glide of my face
when I knelt at the pond.

Chamber of Horrors £2 Extra

Queen Victoria sits in upholstery,
dumb and deflated at the bad news.

One shoulder hunched against the onslaught
of history, King George clenches his fists,
is anxious to be going, perhaps because
his jacket fits badly and his braces show.
His left sleeve is shorter than the right.
His tailor will be shot at dawn.

Somewhere down the corridor, Elvis
has not yet left the building.
Meanwhile, dust gloves the Queen Mum's hands,
Gawbless'er. Diana, in lime-green courtelle
with pintucks, widens her eyes. The little minx—
her hand sneaks towards the Prince's bum.

And poor Charles, he'll never hear her.
Not with those ears. Something has
gone wrong with his hair. He can barely stand.
The whole shooting match is a disgrace.

Who is in charge here? Not the man who
fitted limbs, nor the wigmaker,
window-dresser, property mistress.
Least of all him, smirking in the ticket booth.

Adolf flaps camply at Benito, Kennedy snarls:
they all will fall over when the line dance starts.
And right here in front, all togged up
with spotless boots, is General MacArthur,
the last famous soldier, threatening foreclosure
as Bank Holiday rain strafes the beach.

If anything's right, it's their eyes,
holding them in purgatory until they understand
what's going on in the basement.

The freakshow of visitors passes in a blur.
The last good times were the seventies, where
Michael Jackson is a ten-year old angel.
No one has divorced or died, the mistresses
and massacres all lie ahead
along with Bush, Blair, Bin Laden
on this side of the glass.

The Cambridge Metro

At the Norman Foster Park & Ride,
your iris scan charms the barrier. Take
your place on the moving staircase into
music, the glass drum of the ticket hall.

From Gog Magog to Science Park
on the green line via Drummer Street
(sponsored by Tesco At Addenbrooke's)—
you can go anywhere from here.

Suspended from the ceiling, the escalator drive's
encased in perspex: built in the nineties,
that age of naked fascination
with how things worked. It beckons down

to the platform with its rare mosaic
of recycled circuit boards.
Above you, concrete pillars soar
to somewhere underneath the seventh tee.

Sunlight slices in from where weather is,
igniting sudden colours in your hair—twenty
monitors repixellate. This is
a space of possibility, a nave

transcending transport. Each clean line
sings far above the vox humana.
Coins shine in the busker's cap.
A train sighs in, trailing jewel cases

of academics, tourists, engineers,
and all their somewhere elses.
And you? Will you buy a single
to Lammas Land, years down the line?

You have a wealth of indecisions
as you tap your foot and check the timetable.
Don't imagine, because you're underground
no one cares about your journey

barrelling under the Cam, the vaults and traffic.
Here comes the guard, in his light blue uniform.
You can ask him now what's happening outside.
You may never want to leave.